PUSHKIN'S
FAIRY TALES

PUSHKIN'S FAIRY TALES

Translated by JANET DALLEY   Introduction JOHN BAYLEY

Lithographs ARTHUR BOYD

BARRIE & JENKINS
COMMUNICA - EUROPA

CONTENTS

INTRODUCTION

ushkin is the greatest Russian poet; one of the greatest in world literature. But the term 'poet' means much more in his case than in most, for in a comparatively short life he created masterpieces in practically every genre of literature one can think of – lyric, epic, novel, both in verse and prose, short story, long poetic drama and swift incisive one-act play. And of course the fairy tale – the fairy tale in verse.

The verse is very important, for it determines the *tone* of these fairy tales, which is a unique one. They do not take themselves quite seriously. At the same time there is nothing facetious about them. They are marvellously and economically lyrical, and they induct the reader straight away into a world of fantasy and beauty unlike any other, a world 'smelling of Russia'. The Russian language is inflected, which means that word order is much more flexible than in English; and also that there are many more rhyme words available. Pushkin's octosyllabics, in which much of his best poetry was written, are famous for their perfect control, a simplicity and adroitness like that of the most accomplished prima ballerina, and contriving in the same way to give an impression of being totally natural in the midst of supreme artifice. Pushkin was himself devoted to the ballet, and in his novel in verse, *Evgeny Onegin*, he creates an evocation of Istomina, a St Petersburg ballerina he had often seen; making his verse conform, as it were, to her movements as she flits across the stage.

In the same way there is something ballet-like in the sparkling progress of these *skazki*, or fairy tales. But they are also humorous and homely, with the sort of deadpan humour that is like a good-natured wink. The narrator seems half a poet, like Pushkin, and half a salty humorous old lady, like Pushkin's nurse, Arina Rodionovna, from whom as a boy he heard some of the tales. A lot of them will seem familiar to anyone with a knowledge of fairy stories, for Pushkin's old nurse was not drawing upon some deep mysterious well of Russian folklore, but on recollections and half-remembered fragments transmitted orally by the servants and workers on a Russian estate. Someone who could read had picked them up, most likely, from a dog-eared chap-book translated from a western source.

Of course there is some specifically Russian or Slav material involved. Baba Yaga is a formidable Russian witch, and the water-nymph or *rusalka*, who makes an appearance in the magical prologue, is a creature from Slav folklore, like the nix or undine in German and Swiss mythology. When girls drowned themselves for love they became *rusalki*, and sat on the banks or in the trees above the stream, luring men to their deaths. They seem to have exercised a fascination for Pushkin, who wrote more than one poem in which they figure, as well as an unfinished play. Perhaps they represented for him the power of fate, often a tragic or sardonic theme in his work. The *femme fatale* was certainly a feature of his own life. After many affairs with women, some happy, a few heart-breaking, he married in 1831 a young and singularly beautiful girl, Natalia Goncharovna. The Tsar conceived an admiration for her, and Pushkin, then in his thirties, was made a court page in order that she should be able to attend all the imperial balls. Pushkin had loved the *monde* in his time, but now he was bored dreadfully, and he longed to get away and work in the country. Others too admired his wife, and a French officer called D'Anthès paid her particularly marked attentions. Pushkin did not suspect her of infidelity, but he was determined to end what was becoming an increasingly intolerable situation. He and D'Anthès fought a duel on 27 January 1837, when Petersburg was deep in snow. Pushkin was mortally wounded and died two days later.

He had always worked in fits and starts. Most of the year he would be in Petersburg, gambling, going to parties and seeing his friends. But he always tried to spend the autumn at his small estate at Boldino, where in six weeks or so he would turn out a marvellous great mass of work of every description. It was in one of these Boldino autumns, within a few years of his death, that most of the *skazki* were written; and their cheerfulness and lightness and clear beauty make it all the more ironic that Pushkin at the time was in a dark mood, oppressed by debts and disillusionments, and thoughts of fate and death, which come out in his sombre and powerful play on the Don Juan theme, *The Stone Guest*.

The tone is very different in *Ruslan and Lyudmila*, a long fairy poem Pushkin wrote when he was young, and which both enjoys and 'sends up' the time-honoured stock properties of magic:

Awaking each day from sleep [he writes at the beginning of the fourth canto] I thank God from my heart that in our time magicians are not so numerous as they once were. And therefore our marriages – honour and glory to them – are not so much in danger!

Prophetic words – so with hindsight we may say, thinking of the fate that was to befall Pushkin – but they are uttered in his inimitably light-hearted fashion, playful and worldly without being sophisticated. In the *skazki* the poet intrudes much less, in fact hardly at all, and the fairy-tale elements are simply the facts of life, as natural and homely as the broken wash-trough which is all the fisherman's wife is left with at the end of the tale of the fisherman and the golden fish.

9

All Pushkin's works are in a sense an examination of literary forms: each defines and embodies its own chosen form. So much so that his work was the inspiration of what today in Russia is called 'formalist' criticism, with its thesis that for the reader 'perception of the form reveals the content of the work'. This is certainly true of such light-hearted early poems as *Ruslan and Lyudmila*, whose magical prologue begins this book, and it is also true of a wonderfully funny and irreverent burlesque, the *Gavriliiad*, which relates in epic style how the Virgin Mary is 'visited' by three admirers, the Prince of Darkness, the Archangel Gabriel, and the Holy Ghost.

'What goings-on!' thought Mary, quite worn out. 'The Evil One, an Archangel and God have all possessed me in a single day.'

Another, 'The Tale of Tsar Nikita and His Forty Daughters', is the perfection of what Chaucer would have called a 'lewd tale'. It relates how the beautiful daughters, born without a certain indispensable item of feminine anatomy, none the less manage to acquire it. But the Russian literary establishment, whether tsarist or Soviet, has always been decidedly prudish, and the tale has only come down to us in a sort of *samizdat* version from the memory of Pushkin's younger brother – it is almost impossible to get hold of!

'The Tale of Tsar Saltan', which was the favourite of Prince Mirsky, doyen of Russian literary critics, has indeed the perfection of an archetypal fairy tale, with its adventures, its scenery, and its happy ending. But 'The Tale of the Golden Cockerel', in some ways the most interesting of all the *skazki*, shows that the formalist attitude has its limitations in regard to Pushkin, as it surely must do where all great literature is concerned. For if 'The Tale of a Fisherman and a Golden Fish' has a simple 'moral', that of the Golden Cockerel has a more cryptic atmosphere of irony: it would not be too much to claim that, like Tolstoy's completely realistic tale of power politics, 'Hadji Murad', it also makes its comment in allegorical fashion on the nature of rulers and power. The Tsar Nicholas had always played a cat-and-mouse game with Pushkin, alternately threatening him and acting the part of a gracious patron. In his own text of the poem he substituted 'It's a bad business to pick a quarrel with Tsars' for the more general- ised, 'With some people it's a mistake to pick a quarrel'. There was a kind of meaning here for 'young fellows' – indeed for anyone who had suffered at the hands of authority – and Pushkin's friends probably appreciated the point, just as a Russian under Soviet rule might do today.

There is incidentally, a particular interest in the source of this tale. As I have suggested, Pushkin had a good-natured contempt for the 'folklorists' and the patriots who wanted all such things to be wholly Russian – *echt deutsch* as the Germans say. It would have amused him that a Soviet critic has written a solemn and learned work maintaining that his genius was the simple expression of good working-class Russian nature – via his nurse – and had nothing to do with the effete aristocracy or the bourgeois literature of Europe. In fact Pushkin cared as little as Shakespeare where his stories came from, provided that he could adapt them to his purpose: there is neither reverence nor pedantry in the way he goes about the business. But it is significant that in 1833, the year before he wrote 'The Tale of the Golden Cockerel', he had probably read a French translation of a collection of Arabian Nights-style sketches by the American author Washington Irving, one of which bears a very close resemblance to the plot of his own tale.*

There is a certain piquancy about one of the earliest American authors unknowingly supplying a story to the first and greatest of the Russians. Even more interesting, the warning agent in Washington Irving's tale is not a golden cockerel but a bronze horseman, and in the same year that he wrote the tale Pushkin also produced his poetic masterpiece, *The Bronze Horseman*, a narrative in which a poor clerk is driven mad by the drowning of his fiancée in the great Petersburg flood. The poem is dominated by the gigantic and imperious bronze statue of Peter the Great, which alone continues to tower above the waves engulfing the capital he had created.

I hope this delightful collection of his tales will not only delight the reader but also stimulate him or her to read more of Pushkin's work and find out more about him, for he is certainly one of the most fascinating of writers. Although the translation problem is such a difficult one Janet Dalley has done an excellent job of putting the stories into a lively and effective prose equivalent of Pushkin's untransmittable verses. *Tam chudesa*, as the Prologue says – 'There are wonders . . .'. And one hopes and feels that the 'learned cat' is still stalking round about on his chain, on the green oak by some sea bay, where the waves wash on the shore.

John Bayley
St Catherine's College,
Oxford

*I have written about this in greater detail in my book *Pushkin: A Comparative Commentary* (Cambridge University Press).

PROLOGUE

A green oak stands by the shores of a bay. Around the oak is a golden chain, and day and night a learned cat walks round and round on the chain. As he walks to the right, he sings a song; as he walks to the left, he tells a story.

There are wonders there: a wood-goblin wanders, a sea-nymph sits in the branches. There, on mysterious forest paths, lie the tracks of invisible creatures. A hut with no windows or doors stands on chickens' legs. The hills and and valleys are full of strange visions – There at dawn the waves wash over the sandy and deserted shore; and thirty knights, one by one, come glistening up out of the clear water, attended by their sea-tutor. A prince, passing by, takes as his prisoner a cruel tyrant king; in the clouds, across forests and oceans, a sorcerer carries away a brave young man. In a dark dungeon a princess languishes, with only a brown wolf to be her faithful slave. The great witch Baba Yaga sits in a mortar, which wanders about by itself; King Kashchey, the old miser, sighs over his mounds of gold.

The spirit of Russia is there – a scent of Russia is in the air.

And there I sat, drinking mead. I saw the green oak by the sea, and sat beneath it as the learned cat told me his stories. Some of these I remember, and I will tell them now to the world. . . .

1828

There at dawn the waves wash over the sandy and deserted shore; and thirty knights, one by one, come glistening up out of the clear water

THE TALE OF
THE GOLDEN COCKEREL

Somewhere, in a thrice-nine kingdom, in a thrice-ten state, lived the great Tsar Dadon. In his youth he had been bold and ruthless, and waged terrible wars against the rulers of neighbouring kingdoms – but in his old age he wanted to rest from war, and build a peaceful life. Then the neighbouring rulers started to attack the old king, as viciously as he had done before. To guard the borders of his kingdom he had to maintain a huge army. His officers tried hard, but they just could not succeed – if they were expecting the enemy from the south, the armies would appear from the east. If they were organised against attack on land, the savage intruders would appear from the sea. Tsar Dadon could not sleep; he wept with fury. Life was becoming unbearable. So he turned for help to a sorcerer, an astrologer; he sent a messenger begging him to come to the court.

The sorcerer came up close to Dadon's throne, and pulled from his bag a golden cockerel. 'Take this bird,' he said to the tsar, 'and place it on top of the highest pinnacle. My cockerel will guard you faithfully – as long as all is peaceful, he will sit in silence on the spire. But if there is a threat of war from any side, or forces massed for attack, or any unexpected danger, in a flash the cockerel will raise his crest, spread his wings and crow aloud, and will turn on his spire to face the direction from which danger comes.'

The tsar was delighted with the sorcerer, and made him a promise. 'In return for this favour,' he said, 'I will grant your first wish, whatever it may be, as if it were my own.'

The cockerel kept watch over the kingdom from his high spire. Whenever danger could be seen, the faithful sentry would rouse himself as if from a sleep, spread his wings, and turning towards the danger, cry: 'Cock-a-doodle-doo! Reign in peace, tsar!' And the neighbouring rulers grew quiet, and did not dare to go to war, for Tsar Dadon could now fend them off from all sides.

A year, and then another, went by in peace. The cockerel sat on in silence. Then, one day, Tsar Dadon was awakened by a terrible noise: 'Tsar, your Majesty!' shouted the commander, 'Sir, wake up, please!'

'What's the matter?' asked Dadon, yawning. 'Who's there – what's the trouble?' The commander told him: 'The cockerel is crowing; the whole city is filled with fear and chaos.' The tsar went to the window – he saw that the cockerel had turned on the spire to face the east. There was no time to lose. 'Quickly! Men – to horse! Faster, faster!' The tsar sent out an army to the east, with his eldest son in command. The cockerel calmed down, the clamour quietened, and the tsar settled down again.

Eight days passed, and no news came from the war. No one knew whether or not there had been a battle, and Dadon received no messenger. Then, the cockerel crowed again. The tsar called up another army force, and this time he sent his younger son to the rescue of the elder. The cockerel was silent.

Once again, no news came. And again, eight days passed. The people of the town spent the days in terror . . . then the cockerel shrilled once more. The tsar called up a third army, and himself led them away to the east, not knowing what they would find.

Day and night they moved on; it was becoming unbearable. They found no sign of killing, no camp site, no burial place. A week had already passed, and the tsar was leading his men into the mountains. Suddenly, among the highest peaks, they saw a silken tent. In a narrow mountain pass lay the bodies of the

Suddenly, the silken tent swept open, and a girl, a princess of Shamakhan, shimmering with beauty like the dawn, stepped out to meet the king

At the sight of her, he forgot the death of his sons

Dadon stayed with her in utter entrancement, spellbound

defeated army; men stood around the tent in silent amazement. Tsar Dadon rushed forward – what a terrible sight! Before him his two sons lay dead, without their armour, their swords driven through each other. Their horses wandered loose in the crushed and blood-stained grass. The tsar began to weep: 'My sons, my sons! Both my proud falcons caught in one net! I shall die from grief!' The people began to mourn with their tsar. With a heavy moan the depths of the hills echoed, and the heart of the mountains shook at its foundations.

Suddenly, the silken tent swept open, and a girl, a princess of Shamakhan, shimmering with beauty like the dawn, stepped out to meet the king. Like the birds of night before the sun, the tsar was silenced. At the sight of her, he forgot the death of his sons. She smiled at Dadon – and with a little bow, took his hand and led him into her tent. There she sat him at a table, and feasted him with sumptuous food, and he lay on a bed of brocade. A week passed, as Dadon stayed with her in utter entrancement, spellbound.

At length, Dadon set out on his journey home, with his armies and the young princess. Before them galloped the rumours, spreading both fact and fiction. The townspeople met them at the city gates, with a noisy welcome. Everyone ran behind Dadon and his princess in the royal carriage, and Dadon greeted everyone. Then, in the town, he caught sight of his old friend the sorcerer, whose turbaned head rose in the crowd like the head of a grizzled swan. 'Greetings, old man' called the tsar. 'Come over here and tell me if there is anything you want.' 'Tsar,' replied the wise man, 'do you remember? You promised me that, in return for my favour to you, you would grant the first thing I asked for. So please let me now have the girl, the Shamakhan princess.'

24

'What!' cried Dadon, aghast. 'Either a devil has got into you, or you have lost your senses. What can you be thinking of? Of course I gave you my promise, but everything must have its limits. And remember who I am – ask me rather for a chest of gold, or a noble title, or a horse from the royal stables – ask for half my kingdom!'

'I want none of those. Let me take the Shamakhan princess,' the wise man replied. The tsar spat with fury: 'What an evil man! No, you will get nothing! You have brought trouble on yourself, old man – drag him away!'

The old man wanted to argue in his defence, but with some people it is best not to argue.

Tsar Dadon hit him on the forehead with his staff; the old man fell to the ground, and died. The whole crowd shuddered in horror, but the princess burst into high peals of laughter. The tsar, although he was greatly alarmed, smiled at her. Then, as Dadon was moving on into the town, a sudden slight sound was heard, and the assembled townspeople watched as the cockerel swooped down from the spire, flew to the carriage, and alighted on top of the tsar's head. He spread his wings, pecked once at the tsar's head, and soared up into the sky . . . and Dadon fell from his carriage, sighed once – and died. And the princess vanished, as if she had never existed. . . .

The story isn't true, but there's a hint in it; a lesson for all the young and ruthless.

1834

Tsar Dadon hit him on the forehead with his staff

Dadon fell from his carriage, sighed once – and died

THE TALE OF
A SHE-BEAR

On the pale dawn of a warm spring day, a she-bear wandered out of the dozing wood with her gentle cubs, to roll and look about, and greet the morning.

The she-bear sat beneath a silver birch-tree, while the cubs began to play, rolling on the grass and turning somersaults, wrestling with each other.

None of them noticed the man's approach.

He clutched a long spear in his hands, a knife was tucked into his belt, and he carried a bag on his shoulders.

Suddenly the she-bear sensed the man with the spear.

She began to roar, and call her young ones, her foolish cubs.

'Oh children, my cubs! Stop your games . . . stop your fighting and somersaults – a man has found us. Get up, hide behind me . . . I won't let him take you, I'll fight him. . . .'

The cubs threw themselves behind their mother in sudden terror.

The bear, enraged, reared up on her huge hind legs.

But the man was cunning.

He rushed at the bear, and hurled his spear into her belly – she crashed to the damp ground.

He tore open her belly, and skinned her; he put the baby bears in his bag and set off home.

'Here's a little present for you, wife, to make a bear-skin coat. It must be worth fifty roubles. And here's another present – three cubs, each worth at least five.'

The news travelled quietly through the town, and spread through the forest.

The news reached the great black he-bear.

That the man had slaughtered his mate, and ripped open her white belly, and taken her cubs away in a bag.

The bear began to mourn for her; he hung his head, and howled for his lady, his dark brown she-bear.

'My she-bear, my wife – why have you left me, lonely, widowed. Only with you, my lady, can we play happy games, and bear gentle children, and rock our cubs to sleep.'

The animals started to gather, coming to the bear, the lord of the woods.

The large animals came, and the small creatures came, scampering and running.

A gentlemanly wolf came, with jealous eyes and greedy teeth, loping through the woods.

A fat-tailed beaver, the merchant of the forest, was the next guest.

The weasel, lady-like and dainty; a squirrel, a duchess; the fox, who was the local official – all ran to where the great bear was sitting lost in his sorrow.

The friendly clown, a stoat, came too; and the marmot who lived under the threshing-floor, who was the priest.

A poor, dull-grey doe hare came limping along, and a pious hedgehog.

The hedgehog was all huddled up.

His bristles stood out in sharp, ugly spikes.

1830

He tore open her belly and skinned her

THE TALE OF TSAR SALTAN

ate one night, three girls sat spinning by their window.

'If I were the queen,' said one, 'I'd cook the most sumptuous feasts in the world.'

'If I could be queen,' said her sister, 'I'd weave the finest linen ever seen.'

'If I were queen,' said the third sister, 'I would give the tsar a son who was strong and brave.'

As they spoke, the door opened quietly, and the tsar, the lord of the land, strode into the room. During the conversation he had been standing at the door; the last words he had heard had captivated him.

'My beautiful girl,' he said, 'be my queen, and we shall have a brave, strong son. And you, pretty sisters, leave your cottage and follow me to the palace with your sister. One of you shall be the royal cook, and the other the royal weaver.'

They all set off on the journey to the palace. The tsar didn't waste any time, and that same evening they were married. Tsar Saltan sat by his young queen at the royal feast; then the noble-men led the couple to their ivory bed, and left them. In the kitchen the cook raged with jealousy, and the weaver cried bitterly at her wheel, envying the bride.

There was war in the land at that time. The tsar mounted his battle-horse, and said goodbye to his wife, telling her to take good care of herself and her coming child. While he was still away fighting, the queen had a baby, a son. She cared for him like a mother eagle watching over her young. She sent a messenger to the king with a letter, telling him the good news. But the cook and the weaver, and their mother, were planning to get rid of her, so they sent another messenger in his place, with this message: 'In the night the queen gave birth – not to a son or a daughter, but to a creature which no one has ever seen before, a monster.'

When the tsar heard the news which the messenger had brought, he was furious and ordered the messenger to be hanged. But he calmed down, and instead gave a message in reply: 'Let the queen wait until I come back to make any decisions.'

At last the messenger arrived back. But again the sisters way-laid the man; they made him drunk, and substituted another letter in his pouch. So, later that day, the drunken rider announced this message: 'The tsar orders his nobles to throw the queen and her offspring into the sea. Do this immediately, and do it in secret.'

The nobles didn't dare to disobey. They went to the queen's room, and explained the king's command to her, reading aloud the order containing their horrible duty. Then they put her and her baby in a barrel, sealed it with tar, rolled it away and threw it into the ocean. . . . That was Tsar Saltan's command.

Stars gleamed in the deep blue sky, and the waves pitched in the blue sea; storm-clouds crept across the sky, as the barrel tossed on the ocean. The widow-queen cried bitterly, and beat her hands against the sides of the barrel. . . and the child suddenly began to grow, not by days, but by the hour, bigger and bigger. The day passed as the queen sobbed, but the child spoke to a wave:

'Oh, free blue wave, you can splash wherever you wish, crashing down on the ocean rocks, lifting the ships: don't destroy us – carry us safely on to dry land.'

The wave listened to him, and carried the barrel lightly on to the shore and drew back quietly. The mother and her son were safe, for they could feel the dry land underneath them – but how could they get out of the barrel? The boy got to his feet and pushed his head against the lid of the barrel, straining hard, until he burst open the lid, and they stepped out.

They were free. Looking around they saw a hill with a single green oak on it, standing on a wide plain, and all around the blue sea. The boy realised that they must find some food. He ripped a branch from the oak, and bent it into the shape of a bow, and strung it with the silk cord which held the cross around his neck. He found a fine, slender cane, and used it to make a light arrow; he went towards the beach to look for game over the sea.

Just as he reached the shore, he heard what seemed to be a groan, and noises coming from the sea. He looked about – and saw a horrible sight. A swan was fighting for her life among the pitching waves; a black kite hovered over her, poised in the air, while she splashed helplessly in the churning water. His beak was bloodstained, and his sharp talons were ready to attack again. But at that moment the arrow flew through the air, and struck the great kite in the throat – the huge bird fell, pouring blood into the sea. The prince lowered his bow, and watched as the kite began to sink, with a cry which did not sound like the cry of a bird. The swan swam round, pecking the kite and hurrying its death by beating it with her wings. The big bird sank into the sea. Then the swan spoke to the prince in a human voice:

'Prince, you have saved my life with your only arrow. Because of me you will not be able to get food, but do not worry. I will repay your kindness, and be a good friend to you. It is not a swan that you have saved, but a girl under a spell; you did not kill a bird but a sorcerer. I will never forget you – you may always count on me. Now go back and sleep, and don't worry about what will happen.'

The swan flew away, and the queen and the prince, both famished, lay down to sleep. When the prince opened his eyes in the morning, shaking off the night's dreams, he was astonished to see a large town, with walls with thick battlements, and behind the white walls glistening church domes and the spires of magnificent cloisters. He hurried to wake the queen, who stared in amazement at what she saw. He wondered to himself what would happen next, now that the magic swan had begun to amuse herself!

Mother and son walked to the town. As soon as they reached the gates, a deafening peal of bells rang out, people flocked to greet them, and the church choirs sang. The noblemen came in huge golden carriages to meet them; everyone cheered them loudly. They crowned the prince as their king, and proclaimed him their ruler. So he began his reign in his new-found capital that day, and became known as Prince Guidon.

The wind was playing over the seas as it sped on a small ship, which skimmed over the water with its sails full set. Sailors crowded along the decks, marvelling at the sight of the bare island that they had known – now with a new, golden city on it, and a dock with strong gates. Cannons roared out from the dock, inviting the ship to come ashore. Prince Guidon welcomed the travellers to his palace, and gave them food and drink, and asked what cargo they were carrying, and where they were sailing. The sailors answered:

'We have sailed all over the world, selling precious furs – sable and silver fox – and now it is time for us to return. We sail straight to the east, past the island of Buyan, back to our good Tsar Saltan.'

'Gentlemen,' said the prince. 'I hope your journey will be a quiet one, back to Saltan's kingdom. Please send Saltan my greetings.'

The guests set off again, and Prince Guidon watched them sail

A swan was fighting for her life among the pitching waves

into the distance with sadness. He looked around, and saw the white swan swimming in the choppy water.

'Well, good prince! Why do you look so sad, like a cloudy day? Is something making you unhappy?' she asked him.

The prince answered, 'I feel very sad, because I would so much like to see my father again.'

'Is that all?' said the swan. 'Listen; would you like to fly off and overtake the ship? Turn into a mosquito!' And she flapped her wings, splashing the water noisily, and drenched him from head to foot. Straight away he shrank to the size of a dot and turned into a mosquito – he flew away, buzzing, and overtook the ship at sea. Silently he hid himself in a chink in the boat.

The wind sang happily, and the ship sped past the island of Buyan, to the kingdom of Tsar Saltan – his longed-for country was seen in the distance at last. The men went ashore and the king invited them to his palace. Behind them, into the court, flew our hero. He saw Tsar Saltan sitting in state, crowned and splendid on his throne, with a sad frown on his face. The weaver and the cook, and their wicked mother, sat around the tsar, watching him. He seated his guests at his table, and asked: 'Well, gentlemen – did you sail far? Where did you get to? Was all well, overseas? And what wonders did you find?'

The sailors answered: 'We have been all around the world, and the lands over the seas are peaceful. But we found the most extraordinary thing – there is an island in the ocean which used to be steep and deserted, quite bare. It was an empty land, with only a single oak tree on it – but now a new city with a court, and gilded churches, mansions and gardens, is there. Prince Guidon lives in the palace, and he sends his respects to you.'

Tsar Saltan was astonished, and said: 'If I live long enough, I must visit this wonderful island, and stay with Guidon for a time.'

The two sisters and their mother didn't want Saltan to go off to find the magic island.

'How miraculous . . .' said the cook sarcastically, winking at the others. 'So there's a city in the ocean! I know of a thing which is much more surprising: somewhere in a wood there stands a fir-tree, and underneath it a small squirrel sings songs, cracking nuts all day – but these are no ordinary nuts. Each nutshell is made of gold, and inside the kernels are pure emeralds. That's what I call a marvellous thing.'

The tsar was astonished by this new story; but the mosquito was furious. He flew up to his aunt and stung her in the right eye. The cook turned white, and fainted – and never saw from that eye again. Her sister, her mother and the serving-maids began to chase the mosquito, shrieking – 'You wretched insect, you! Wait till we get you!' But he had already flown out of the window, and peacefully away across the sea to his own country.

The prince was walking along the shore, slowly, without lifting his eyes from the water. Again the white swan appeared, bobbing on the current.

'Well, my fair prince! Why do you look so sad again, overcast like a cloudy day? Are you unhappy?' she asked him.

Guidon replied: 'Something is making me sad – I have heard of a wonderful thing that I would like to see. Somewhere in a wood there stands a fir-tree, with a little squirrel under it who sings songs all day, cracking nuts that have shells of gold, and kernels of pure emeralds . . . but I don't know if this can be true.'

The swan answered: 'What people say about the squirrel is

He flew up to his aunt and stung her in the right eye

true – I know where it is. Don't be sad, prince, I'm glad to do this small favour for you.'

The prince went home cheerfully. As he reached the wide courtyard – look! Beneath a tall fir sat a tiny squirrel, cracking the golden nuts and tossing out the emeralds inside, sweeping the shells into a little pile with her tail. All the people and noblemen of the town had gathered to watch her, as she whistled a scrap of song. Awestruck, Guidon whispered: 'Thank you, my friend, and may you have as much happiness as I have.' He built a crystal house for the squirrel, and set a guard over her, and made a scribe keep count of every shell. So the squirrel's fame, and the prince's riches, grew.

The wind was playing over the seas as it sped on a small ship. The sails were set full, and it skimmed quickly over the waves, past the steep island, past the great city – cannons roared out from the dock again, inviting the ship into harbour. The visitors came up to the gates, and Guidon invited them to eat and drink with him, and asked what they had for sale, and where they were going.

'We've travelled all over the world,' the sailors replied, 'selling horses, stallions from the Don country; now it is time for us to to turn for home, for we still have a long way to go – past the island of Buyan, back to our Tsar Saltan.'

The prince wished them a successful journey, and asked them to send his greetings to their tsar.

The guests bowed, and went on their way. The prince walked down to the shore – and there was the swan, waiting for him. He told her that he was longing to see his native land again . . . in a flash she transformed him once more. This time he became a fly, and

44

flew off to overtake the ship, and hide away in its side.

The wind sang happily, and the ship sped past the island of Buyan, back towards Tsar Saltan – the longed-for country could be seen in the distance. The men went ashore, and Saltan invited them to his palace. Behind them, once again, the prince flew into the court. He saw his father sitting in splendour, looking sad and troubled, and around him sat the weaver, the one-eyed cook, and their mother, glaring at him. Saltan greeted his guests, and asked them where they had been, and what they had found over the seas.

'We have sailed all over the world,' answered the visitors, 'and the countries over the seas are at peace. But we did see an extraordinary sight, when we visited the island lying in the ocean, with its golden churches, mansions and gardens. In front of the palace stands a fir-tree, where a nimble squirrel lives in a house made of crystal. She sings strange songs, and cracks nuts whose shells are golden, with kernels of pure emeralds. She has servants to wait on her, and a guard keeps watch. A strict count is made of each nut; from each shell they make a golden coin, and young girls store the emeralds away in caskets. Everyone on the island is rich and they live in fine houses, not in huts. Prince Guidon reigns there, and he sent you his greetings.'

The tsar was amazed: 'If I live long enough, I must visit this island and stay with Prince Guidon.'

But again the cook and the weaver and their mother wanted to stop Saltan from visiting the island. Laughing slyly, the weaver said to the tsar:

'So what? A squirrel cracking nuts, heaping up gold and emeralds – I don't see anything strange about that! Whether it is true or not, I know of a much more wonderful story. There is a

45

place where the sea crashes wildly, boiling and thundering, swishing over a bleak shore; it sucks back again, and leaves behind it on the beach thirty-three knights, tall and strong, in glistening scaly armour. Each is exactly like all the others, all huge and young; with them goes their leader, Chornomor. It's a strange and wild story, but you can be sure it is true!'

The guests were wise enough to be silent, and not argue with her. Saltan was astonished; Guidon, though, became very angry – he buzzed about and settled on his aunt's left eye. The weaver turned pale, and cried out; for now she too was blinded in one eye. Everyone shouted for the fly to be caught . . . but the prince had already flown out of the window, back across the sea to his own kingdom.

The prince wandered gloomily along the shore, staring down at the blue water. Once again, he saw the white swan swimming on the rippling waves.

'Hello again, prince! Why are you so subdued, like a cloudy day? Is something still saddening you?' she asked.

The prince answered her: 'Sadness is troubling me, because I have heard of something miraculous that I would love to see.'

'And what is it?'

'There is a place where the sea swells and crashes, lifting the waves high and washing over a bare shore. As the waves surge back, they leave behind thirty-three knights in armour shining like fire, all handsome and young, all alike, and with them is their leader Chornomor.'

The swan said: 'Is this what is troubling you, prince? Don't be sad, my friend. I know about this – these sea-knights are my blood-brothers. So go home, and wait to greet my brothers as your guests.'

The prince went away, his sadness forgotten. He climbed up to the top of his tower, and sat watching the sea. As he waited the sea began to swirl and rise up, and a sparkling, noisy wave washed over the shore, leaving behind it the thirty-three knights in fiery shining armour, marching up two by two. In front of them walked the silver-haired leader, leading them to the city. Prince Guidon rushed down from the tower to meet them, and the townspeople came running too. Their leader said to the prince:

'The swan sent us to you; she asked us to be the guards of your beautiful city. From now on, we shall march up out of the sea every day to stand guard by your great walls. So, we shall meet again soon, but now we must return to the sea. The air of the land is difficult for us.'

As they had come, so they went back to their sea-home.

The wind was playing over the sea, and tossing a ship in full sail over the waves, past the steep island, past the great city – cannons roared out from the dock to welcome the visitors. When the sailors reached the city gates, Guidon invited them to his palace to eat and drink with him. He asked them where they were sailing, and what merchandise they were carrying. They replied:

'We have sailed across the world, trading in swords of fine steel, and pure silver and gold, but now we must start our long journey home to the east, past the island of Buyan, back to the kingdom of Tsar Saltan.'

The prince said: 'I wish you a safe journey home to Tsar Saltan's country. Please send him my greetings.'

When the guests had left to start their journey, the prince ran down to the shore again – and again the swan was waiting for him. He asked her to let him follow the ship, and she transformed him as she had before. Once again he became very small, and turned into a bee, and flew away buzzing until he overtook the sailing ship, and quietly hid himself in a chink in its side.

The wind sang happily as it blew the ship quickly past the island of Buyan, towards the kingdom of Tsar Saltan – and now his own country could be seen again in the distance. Once ashore, the sailors were invited to Saltan's court, and the bee flew in behind them. There was his father, the tsar, sitting in state, looking sad and miserable, with the cook, the weaver and their mother seated about him, with only four eyes between the three of them. Saltan seated his guests around him, and as usual asked them about their travels.

'We sailed across the world,' the sailors replied, 'and the lands over the seas are peaceful. We saw something most remarkable, on the island in the ocean on which the great city stands. There, every day, the sea surges up, lifting a great wave which floods over the shore leaving behind it thirty-three knights in glistening armour, all fine and young, tall and strong, exactly alike. Their old leader, Chornomor, leads them two by two out of the water to stand guard over the island – they are brave and faithful guards. Prince Guidon reigns there, and once again he sent you his greetings.'

Saltan exclaimed: 'If I live long enough, I shall visit this miraculous island, and be the prince's guest.'

The cook and the weaver didn't say a word, but Babarikha, their mother, roared with laughter and said: 'Who's surprised by this story? Men come out of the sea and wander about as guards? Whether he's telling the truth or not, I don't see what's so remarkable about it. I'll tell you something that is true: far across the seas there is a princess who is so beautiful that none can tear their

eyes from her. By day she outshines the sun in the sky, and at
night she lights up the earth with her beauty. A crescent moon
shines in her hair, and a star sparkles on her forehead; she is sweet,
and walks straight and proud like a peacock, and she speaks like
the rippling music of a stream. I know this is true, and that *is*
something wonderful.'

The wise guests were quiet, as they didn't want to argue with
the old woman. The tsar once again was amazed by this new tale,
but the prince was very angry. He thought he should spare the
old woman's eyes, so he buzzed and circled around her, and
settled on the end of her nose. He stung her nose hard, and
immediately a big blister swelled up on it. Once again there was
chaos in the room:

'Help, help! Guards! Catch it . . . kill it . . .! There it is – no,
wait . . . there!' But the bee had already flown through the window, making his way peacefully back to his own kingdom.

Walking by the sea again, sad and thoughtful, gazing at the water,
the prince again found the white swan floating on the ripples. She
asked him why he seemed so sad.

'A great sorrow is eating at my heart,' he answered. 'People
marry, and I am alone without a wife.'

'And whom do you want to marry?'

'I have heard of a princess somewhere in the world who is so
beautiful that people can hardly tear their eyes away from her. In
the daytime she outshines the sun, and at night she lights up the
earth – a crescent moon glimmers in her hair, and a star sparkles
on her forehead. She walks proud in her beauty like a peacock;
she talks like the musical rippling of a stream. But I wonder: is
this story true?'

He waited anxiously for an answer. The white swan was silent for a moment, thinking. Then she said slowly:

'Yes, there is such a girl. But remember that a wife is not a possession like a mitten, that you can throw away, or tuck into your belt, and treat however you please. Listen to my advice – think hard about this now, so that you don't regret it later.'

The prince assured her that he had thought of this before, and thought hard about it, for he had been thinking of getting married for some time. He swore that he was ready to walk round the world twenty times for the sake of the beautiful princess. The swan sighed, and murmured:

'Why so far? You know, your bride is very near by. This princess is – myself.' Unfolding her wings, she flew over the waves, and landed high up on the shore by a small tree. She shook out her wings, and began to tremble all over; slowly, she turned into a woman. A crescent moon gleamed in her hair, and a star shone on her forehead, she was majestic; when she spoke it was like the gentle music of a stream.

The prince put his arms around her, holding his princess to him. Then he led her to his mother, and asked for her blessing on their marriage.

Over their bowed heads, the queen took the holy icon in her hands, weeping, and blessed them.

The prince did not lose any time in marrying the princess, and they began to live happily together.

The wind was playing over the sea as it sped on a small ship, with sails set full. It skimmed over the waves, past the steep island and the great city. From the dock the cannons roared out to invite the ship into port. Guidon called the sailors to his palace to eat and drink with him, asking them what goods they were carrying and where they were sailing.

They replied: 'We have travelled all over the world, dealing in smuggled goods. We still have a long journey ahead of us, to the east, past the island of Buyan, back to our great king Saltan.'

Guidon said to them: 'Have a pleasant journey, gentlemen, over the seas back to your great king. Please remind him that he has promised to visit my kingdom, and he has not been here yet. Send him my respects.'

The sailors went on their way, but this time Prince Guidon stayed at home with his young wife.

The wind sang happily as the ship sailed past the island of Buyan to Tsar Saltan's kingdom. The familiar land was now in sight. The sailors landed, and the tsar invited them to be his guests. They saw the tsar sitting in splendour in his palace, with the two sisters and their old mother around him, with four eyes between the three of them. Tsar Saltan settled the guests around his throne and asked:

'Well, gentlemen, have you travelled far? Tell me how the lands over the seas are, and what you found there that was interesting.'

The sailors replied: 'We sailed right around the world, and everywhere was peaceful. We saw the island in the sea where the great city with golden churches stands. There is a magic squirrel who lives in a crystal house under a fir-tree in front of the palace. All day it sings little songs, and cracks the nuts with shells made of gold and kernels of pure emeralds. They care for the squirrel, and guard her. And we saw another extraordinary thing happen there. The sea surges up, lifting a huge wave over the empty shore, and leaves behind thirty-three knights in fiery armour, and their leader Chornomor. They are the faithful guards of the island. The prince has a wife so beautiful that none can take their eyes from her; by day she outshines the sun, while at night she lights up the earth around her. In her hair shines a crescent moon, and a star sparkles on her forehead. Prince Guidon reigns in the city. He sent you his greetings, and reproached you for not having come to visit him yet.'

The tsar couldn't wait any longer; he gave the order for his fleet to get ready for the journey to the magic island. The cook and the weaver and their old mother tried again to stop him, as they didn't want him to go. Saltan paid them no attention this time, and made them keep quiet.

'Am I a tsar, or a child?' he said angrily. 'I will set off today.' And he stamped his foot, and went out slamming the door.

Guidon sat by his window, gazing in silence at the sea. It was quiet and smooth, barely rippling. In the blue distance, a boat appeared, then another – Tsar Saltan's fleet was sailing across the smooth sea. Prince Guidon leapt to his feet, and shouted for his mother and his wife to come and look. The fleet was already coming near the island; Guidon took his telescope. The tsar was standing on deck, looking at them through his own telescope. The cook and the weaver, and their mother Babarikha, were with him, staring at this new land.

The cannons roared out a welcome, and the church bells pealed and rang. Guidon walked down to the shore and met the tsar, with the cook, the weaver and their mother. He led the tsar into his city in silence.

They all came up to the palace. By the gate the sentries' armour flashed, and the tsar saw in front of him thirty-three knights, all young and strong, exactly alike, with Chornomor, their leader. As the tsar stepped into the wide courtyard, there beneath a tall fir sat the little squirrel, singing softly, cracking the golden nuts and taking out the emeralds. She put them in a little bag, while the golden shells lay strewn around the courtyard.

The visitors went inside, and met the beautiful princess, with the moon shining in her hair and the star glittering on her forehead, sweet and gracious. Beside her stood her mother-in-law. The tsar looked at her, and suddenly he recognised the wife he had lost; his heart began to pound.

'What do I see? Is it really you?' he gasped, with tears running down his face. The tsar embraced his wife, and his son, and the young princess, and they all sat down to a feast to celebrate.

The weaver, the cook and their old mother Babarikha ran away to hide themselves, but they were pulled out from the corners where they were hiding. They confessed everything that they had done, and begged to be forgiven. The tsar, since he was feeling so happy, simply sent all three home.

The day continued, and finally Tsar Saltan was put to bed, rather drunk.

And I was there, drinking beer and mead, and hardly wet my moustache.

1831

THE TALE OF
A DEAD PRINCESS
AND SEVEN GIANTS

A king said goodbye to his wife and set out on a long journey. The queen sat alone at the window to wait for him. She watched and waited, and gazed at the fields around, from the white dawn until night fell, until her eyes became sore – but there was no sign of her husband. All she saw were the snow-storms whirling up, and snow pouring down on the fields, and as the days passed the earth turned white. Nine months passed, and she never took her eyes from the white land. Then, on Christmas Eve, in the middle of the night, she gave birth to a baby daughter.

Very early that morning, the king, for whom she had waited so long, came home at last from his journey. She gazed at him in delight, and sighed deeply – but the joy and shock were too much for the fragile queen, and she died that day.

For a long time the king was terribly sad. A year passed like an empty dream and then, being human, he married someone else. Certainly his new wife looked like a queen: she was tall and slender, beautiful, and intelligent. But she was proud and very vain; she was self-satisfied and jealous.

The new queen had been given a mirror as a wedding present, and this mirror had a peculiar quality: it could talk.

When she was alone with her mirror she was light-hearted and gentle – she would whisper to it, blushing:

'My friend, my mirror! Talk to me . . . tell me, in all truth: am I the sweetest and fairest woman in the world?'

And the mirror replied: 'Of course, my queen, there is no question. You are the sweetest and fairest of all.'

Then the queen would laugh, and shrug her shoulders, and wink, and snap her fingers, and swing around with her hands on her hips, admiring herself in the mirror.

All this time, the young princess was growing up, quietly emerging as a beauty – fair-skinned with dark eyes, and gentle. She found a husband, whose name was Prince Elysee. The matchmaker came to see the king, who agreed to the wedding, and prepared his daughter's dowry: he gave the couple seven merchant towns, and one hundred and forty castles.

As people began to gather for the wedding celebrations, the queen was standing excitedly in front of her mirror:

'Tell me, mirror, am I the sweetest and fairest woman in the world?'

But the mirror replied:

'You are beautiful, there is no doubt. But the young princess is the sweetest and fairest of all.'

The queen jumped up and waved her arms in fury. She flung the mirror to the ground, and stamped her foot.

'Loathsome mirror! . . . How can you compare her with me? It's not surprising that she's so pale, since her mother did nothing but gaze out at the snow! Oh, how can she be sweeter than me? . . . Don't you know that I am more beautiful than anyone? Look throughout the kingdom, the whole world if you like, but you won't find anyone to equal *me*!'

But the mirror just replied: 'The princess is the sweetest and fairest of all.'

The queen could do nothing to make it change its answer. Full of jealousy and hate, she dashed the mirror to the floor and shouted for Chernavka, her servant-girl. She ordered her to take the princess deep into the woods and leave her tied up underneath a pine tree, so that she would be eaten by the wolves.

(Perhaps this woman was controlled by the devil.)

55

She gazed at him in delight, and sighed deeply – but the joy and shock were too much for the fragile queen, and she died that day

'Of course, my queen, there is no question. You are the sweetest and fairest of all'

She ordered her to take the princess deep into the woods and leave her tied up underneath a pine tree, so that she would be eaten by the wolves

Chernavka went into the woods with the princess, and she led her so far that the princess began to suspect something, and was very frightened.

'What have I done wrong?' she cried out. 'Don't hurt me, please, and when I am a queen I will remember you.'

The girl had a kind heart, so she didn't tie the princess up as she had been told, but let her go and said: 'Don't be too sad – God be with you.'

Then she ran off home.

'Well?' asked the queen. 'Where's the beautiful princess?'

'Out in the forest,' replied the girl. 'Her elbows are tied up tightly, and she will be killed by the claws of the animals. She'll die quickly.'

Word began to go around that the king's daughter was dead. The poor king was very sad, and grieved for his daughter; but Prince Elysee nevertheless set out to search for his beautiful young bride.

The young girl had been wandering in the forest since dawn. She walked and walked, and finally she came to a castle. A small dog came running out to meet her, barking loudly at first, then becoming quiet and playful. She went through the gates into the silent courtyard, and the dog ran behind her affectionately. The princess crept up to the porch, and taking the great ring on the door in her hands, opened it silently. She went into a room with benches all around it covered with blankets. Under the holy icon stood a wooden table, and there was a tiled stove with a bed over it . . . the girl felt that it was the house of people who were kind, and she knew they would do her no harm. But there was no one to be seen. The princess went around the house, and tidied everything. She lit a candle under the icon, and kindled the stove until it was warm. Then she climbed up to the place between the top of the stove and the ceiling, where boards are laid to sleep on, and lay down to rest.

It was nearly supper-time; a tramp of feet could be heard coming through the courtyard. Seven giants, large red-faced young men with whiskers, came in one by one.

'What has happened?' exclaimed the oldest. 'Everything is so neat and clean. Someone has come into the castle while we were out, and is waiting to see who lives here. Who can it be? If it's an old man, he'll be like an uncle to us. If it's an old woman we'll treat her like a mother. If it's a young man, he can be like another brother – and if a pretty young girl, she'll be like our sister.'

The princess came out to meet them, and greeted them, bowing. She blushed, and excused herself for coming into their house unknown and uninvited. Very quickly, they found out what had happened to the princess, and welcomed her; they sat her in a corner by the fire, and brought her some pie and a glass of vodka on a tray. She refused the vodka, and hardly crumbled the pie, only eating a tiny piece – tired from her journey, she asked to go to bed. They led her upstairs, and left her to sleep.

Day after day flashed past, and the young princess was content to live deep in the wood with the seven giants. Before dawn every day, the brothers set off in a noisy, friendly crowd. They would walk in the woods, or chase magpies from the fields, and sometimes shoot the wild grey ducks. Sometimes, too, they fought their enemies – the broad-shouldered Tartars – or drove the Circassians out of the forest. And the princess, meanwhile, kept house by herself in the castle, cleaning and cooking. She didn't contradict them in whatever they did, and they in turn let her do as she wished. The days passed.

The seven brothers were very fond of the young girl. One day, just after dawn, all seven of them went to talk to her in her room. The eldest began:

'You know that we all love you like a sister, but any of us would be glad to marry you – choose one of us, and be his wife . . . why are you shaking your head? Do you refuse?'

'Oh, you are all like brothers to me,' the princess said. 'What can I do? I am engaged to someone else. For me you are all equal, all brave, all intelligent, and I love you all from my heart. But I have already promised to marry someone, and for me, Prince Elysee is the most precious.'

The brothers stood about in silence, and scratched their heads awkwardly.

'Well, there was no harm in asking. Forgive us,' said the eldest, bowing. 'Let it be as if we had never mentioned it.'

'I am not angry,' she said quietly, 'and my refusal should not be taken amiss.'

The young men bowed to her, and went away quietly; once again they were all agreed to live and let live.

Meanwhile, the wicked queen couldn't stop thinking about the princess, and spent long hours sulking and raging at her mirror. Finally she got tired of this and sat down in front of it, forgetting her anger, and began to show off again. With a smile she said:

'Mirror! Tell me, now, tell me the truth: am I the sweetest and fairest woman in the world?'

And the mirror replied:

'You are beautiful, there is no doubt; but, far from here in the green oak forest, unnoticed by the world, in the house of seven giants lives the girl who is sweeter than you.'

The queen flew to Chernavka in a rage:

'How dare you betray me?!' she screamed.

The girl was so frightened that she confessed everything. The wicked queen threatened her with a dagger, telling her that if she did not find a way to kill the princess, she herself would die.

The princess was sitting at the window, spinning, and waiting for the brothers to come home. Suddenly, outside the window, the little dog began to bark furiously. The girl looked out, and saw a beggar woman dressed in black come in to the courtyard, fending off the dog with her crutch.

'Wait, old woman, wait a minute,' she called to her from the window. 'I'll come and hold the dog, and bring something for you.'

The beggar woman replied: 'Oh lady! This wretched dog is worrying himself to death. Look, what a fuss he's making! It must be because of me.'

The princess started to go out to give her some bread, but she had hardly left the porch when the dog hurled himself under her feet in a frenzy of barking. He would not let her go up to the old woman, nor the old woman to her.

'I don't know what is the matter with him,' the princess said to her. 'Here, catch!' and she threw the bread.

The little old woman caught the bread.

The girl looked out, and saw a beggar woman dressed in black come in to the courtyard, fending off the dog with her crutch

'Bless you,' she said, 'God bless you, my dear. This is for you – catch!' And to the princess she threw a juicy, young, golden apple. The dog leapt in the air, and began to squeal – but the princess grabbed the apple in both hands.

'Taste the apple, my dear. You will like it. And bless you for the food,' the old woman bowed to the princess, and disappeared.

The dog ran into the porch with the princess and gazed sadly into her face, whining softly. He wanted to tell her to throw away the apple, but he could not. She stroked him gently: 'Well, Sokolka, what is the matter with you?' – and went in to her room, shutting the door. She sat down by the window, at her spinning-wheel, to wait for the brothers. Her eyes kept straying to the apple.

It was full of ripe juice, so fresh and so fragrant, so rosy-golden – as if honey had been poured over it! You could almost see the pips inside. . . .

She couldn't bear to wait until supper-time. She took the apple and lifted it to her lips, quietly took a little taste, swallowed a morsel. Suddenly she staggered, breathless; her white hands dropped, and the rosy fruit fell to the floor . . . her eyes rolled, and she fell, her head on the bench beneath the icon. She lay still.

At that moment, the seven brothers were walking home in a boisterous crowd, laughing and playful. The dog rushed out along the path to meet them, his tail between his legs, howling terribly; they realised that some disaster had happened. They ran in to the house, and gasped in shock at what they saw. Running after them, the dog hurled himself on the apple, with a furious yelp. He ate the apple in a single gulp, collapsed on the floor and died. It had been filled with poison.

The brothers lowered their heads in sadness, and gently lifted the princess from the bench and laid her out carefully. They wanted to bury her, but they hesitated – she was lying so quietly, so freshly, as if under the wings of sleep, but she was not breathing. They waited three days, but the princess didn't wake up.

They said quiet, sad prayers over her body, then laid her in a crystal coffin, and carried it at midnight to a deserted mountain. Carefully they fixed the coffin on iron chains hung from six columns, and put railings around it to guard it. Making a deep bow before their dead sister, the eldest of the brothers said:

'Sleep in peace in your crystal coffin. Your beauty has been extinguished by some terrible evil; your soul has been claimed by heaven. We loved you – so we have buried you where no one can ever find you.'

The same day the wicked queen, waiting for the good news, took her mirror secretly, and asked it again: 'Tell me, am I the sweetest and the fairest woman of all?'

And she heard in reply: 'You, queen, you are the sweetest and fairest in the world.'

Prince Elysee, in the meantime, had been searching the land for his fiancée. She was nowhere to be found. He cried bitterly; whoever he asked found his questions puzzling, and no one wanted to meet his eyes, but turned away quickly. Finally the young man turned to the great red sun.

'Bright sun! You can cross the round world through the sky, you lead winter into warm spring; you see us all below you. Please answer me – have you seen the young princess anywhere in the world? I am in love with her.'

They said quiet, sad prayers over her body, then laid her in a crystal coffin

'Bright sun! You can cross the round world through the sky, you lead winter into warm spring; you see us all below you. Please answer me – have you seen the young princess anywhere in the world? I am in love with her'

'My dear boy,' answered the sun, 'I haven't seen the princess. You know, I don't think she is alive. But perhaps the moon, my neighbour, has met her somewhere, or seen some trace of her.'

Elysee waited anxiously on a dark night. When the moon came in sight, he chased after it to make his inquiry:

'Moon, moon, my friend! You gleam golden in the sky! You rise in the deep darkness, round-faced and bright-eyed, as the stars gaze at you. Surely you can help me – have you seen the young princess anywhere in the world? I am in love with her.'

'My friend,' answered the bright moon, 'I haven't seen the lovely girl. I only stand guard in my turn, at night. She may have passed by when I was not there.'

'What can I do?' cried the prince.

'Wait a minute. Perhaps the wind will know something of her. Go to him – he will help you. Don't lose hope – goodbye.'

Elysee ran to find the wind, calling: 'Wind, wind, where are you? You are so powerful; you can drive the storm-clouds and ruffle the blue seas, you can wander everywhere in space, afraid of no one. Please tell me – have you seen the young princess anywhere in the world? I am in love with her.'

'Be patient,' answered the wild wind, 'and listen. There is a high mountain beside a quiet flowing stream, in a deserted place where no footsteps can be seen. In the mountain there is a deep pit, and there, in darkest gloom, you will find a crystal coffin hung on chains between six pillars. In that coffin lies your beloved.'

The wind whirled away. The prince began to sob. He rode away to find this desolate place, to see his beautiful girl once more. He arrived at the foot of the steep mountain, which rose up before him, bleak and deserted. He saw the entrance to the dark pit; quickly, he went inside. Before him in the darkness the crystal coffin was suspended, and inside it lay the princess in her eternal sleep. Overcome with anger and sorrow, he hit out with all his strength at the coffin – it shattered in pieces. Suddenly, the girl came to life. She looked about her slowly, with amazement in her eyes and, still swaying on the chains which held the coffin, she stretched and sighed. 'I have slept for such a long time!' She rose out of the coffin.

They were both overjoyed. He took her in his arms and carried her out of the darkness into the light. As they set off on the return journey, the news was already spreading: the king's daughter was alive!

The evil stepmother was sitting idly at home in front of her mirror, chatting to it. 'Am I the sweetest and fairest woman in the world?' she asked.

And she heard the reply: 'You are beautiful, there is no doubt. But the young princess is the sweetest and fairest of all.'

The wicked woman jumped up, smashed the mirror to the floor, rushed out of the room – and ran straight into the princess. The sight of her made the queen fall down dead with guilt and anguish.

So she was buried, and the wedding took place. Elysee and his princess were blessed. No one since the world began had seen such a feast.

I was there, drinking mead and beer, and hardly wet my moustache.

1833

'Wind, wind, where are you? You are so powerful ; you can drive the storm-clouds and ruffle the blue seas, you can wander everywhere in space, afraid of no one. Please tell me – have you seen the young princess anywhere in the world? I am in love with her'

Suddenly, the girl came to life

The sight of her made the queen fall down dead with guilt and anguish

THE STORY OF
A PRIEST AND
HIS SERVANT BALDA

Once there lived a foolish priest. He went to the market-place one day, to look at the goods, and met Balda, who was wandering about with nothing to do.

'Well, old man, you're up early. Is something bothering you?'

'I need a servant,' the priest replied, 'to be my cook, stable-boy, and carpenter. But where am I to find a servant who is not too expensive?'

Balda said: 'I'll be a good servant for you – I work hard and I'm careful. If you feed me well, I'll work for you for a whole year without any reward, except the right to give you three knocks on the head when the year is over.'

The priest thought for a while, scratching his head a little. Knocks on the head, he thought, are surely not always very hard, so he decided to trust his canny nature. 'All right,' he said to Balda. 'We'll both be no worse off. Come and live with me, and show me how hard you can work.'

Balda went to live in the priest's house. He slept on straw, ate enough for four men and worked like seven. From dawn onwards everything was humming – he harnessed the horse, ploughed the field, kindled the stove, prepared the food, stocked the larder – even boiled eggs and shelled them himself. He made the porridge and was nanny to the children. The priest's wife was full of his praises, the priest's daughter adored him, and the priest's son called him Uncle.

It was only the priest who didn't like Balda. He never treated him kindly, and he had begun to worry about letting Balda have his reward when the year had passed.

Time went on; the year had almost come to an end. The priest could not eat or drink for worry, and didn't sleep at night – his head was splitting for weeks beforehand. So he confessed to his wife, and asked her what he could do. The old lady's wits were very sharp, and she knew all sorts of cunning tricks. She said:

'I think I know a way to get out of this. Tell Balda to perform some errand that you know is impossible, and insist that he fulfil it exactly, in return for his wages. Then you will be able to save yourself getting knocked on the head, and send Balda away without his reward.'

The priest began to feel happier; he was able to look Balda in eye again. He thought for a while. Then, he shouted:

'Come here, Balda, my faithful servant. Now listen to me. Long ago, I mortgaged my soul to the devils, and they are supposed to pay me a ransom for it during my life – but they are in arrears, and haven't paid me at all for three years. Go and collect my full dues from the devils, and then you will be able to have your wages.'

Balda started to argue with the priest, but it was no use. He went and sat by the sea-shore. He started to twist a piece of rope tightly between his fingers, and then slapped the water with it fiercely.

An old demon rose slowly out of the water.

'Balda, why have you come here?' he roared.

'I was ruffling the water with my piece of rope to summon you up from the depths, you and your horrible tribe.'

The old demon was hurt by this remark. 'Tell me, why are you being so unkind?'

'What do you mean – why? You haven't paid your dues to the priest or remembered the date when the time was up – so now I'm going to have some fun, and be as much of a nuisance to you as I can!'

'Dear Balda, don't be impatient. You'll have the money in full very soon. Just wait, and I'll send my grandson up to you.'

Balda thought to himself: 'He's not going to fool me with this trick. . . .'

The little demon who was sent up emerged from the water, and began to mew like a kitten. 'Hello, Balda. Why do you need your money? We hadn't heard about it for ages, so all the devils had forgotten about it. Oh well – you can have it . . . but let's agree on one condition, so that neither of us will be upset. Whichever of us can run around the world, across the seas, and return here first, will take the whole ransom. In the meantime they'll prepare the bag of money here.'

Balda burst out laughing, but he was thinking slyly. 'What a stupid idea,' he said. 'How can you compete with me – you are much too small to race against Balda! Wait a minute, and I'll go and fetch my little brother.'

Balda ran off to a near-by wood, and caught two hares, which he put in a bag. He went back to the sea-shore, and found the imp waiting for him.

'You, little imp, are just an infant, a mere stripling – it would only be a waste of time to race against me. Try and outrun my little brother first.' And he held up one of the hares by the ears. 'One, two, three – go!'

The imp and the hare set off: the imp raced along the under-water paths he knew, and the hare dashed straight back to its home in the woods.

When he had run right around the world through the seas, the imp came rushing back, a little wet thing, drying himself with his paw, his tongue stuck out and his snout in the air, out of breath. He was thinking to himself that he had settled the business with Balda beyond a doubt. Then he looked up – and saw Balda's brother! Balda was stroking him and saying: 'Poor little brother, you are very tired. Have a rest now.'

The imp was struck dumb with surprise – he put his tail between his legs, miserable and sulky. He looked sideways at Balda's brother. 'Wait a minute,' he said finally. 'I'll go and get the ransom.'

He went to his grandfather and explained that Balda's younger brother had beaten him in the race. The old demon became very thoughtful. But Balda didn't give him time to think; he was making so much noise from the shore that the whole sea was troubled, and great waves raged around.

So the imp emerged again. 'All right, my friend. We'll send you the whole ransom. Only listen . . . do you see this stick? Choose your favourite position. Whoever can throw this stick the furthest, will take the money. What's the matter? Are you afraid of dislocating your arm? What are you waiting for?'

'I'm waiting for that little storm-cloud over there,' Balda replied. 'When it passes overhead I'll throw the stick into it, and start a tempest that you can't handle, you devils.'

The imp was terrified, and went back again to his grandfather to tell him what had happened. But again Balda made a fearful noise upon the water with his rope, challenging the devils to appear.

The imp appeared again: 'Why are you so fidgety? You'll get the money, as you asked. . . .'

'No,' said Balda. 'Now it's my turn to choose a test. I'll set you a task, young enemy, that will show just how strong you are. Do you see the grey mare in the field over there? Go and pick her up, and carry her half a mile – if you do, you get the ransom money; if not, I get it all.'

The poor young devil bent down under the horse. He strained

and heaved, using all the strength in his back to lift the mare. He lifted her barely from the ground, and staggered a couple of steps. On his third step he fell flat, his legs stretched out in front of him.

Balda said to him scornfully: 'You silly creature! What are you lying down for? You can't even carry the horse in your arms; but look – I can carry her even with my legs.'

And Balda leapt on to the mare's back, and cantered off on her for about a mile, sending up a column of dust.

This time the imp was very frightened. He went off to tell his grandfather about Balda's strange powers. There was nothing to be done – the devils collected together the ransom money, and loaded the sack on to Balda's back. Balda set off, grunting now and then under the weight of it.

When the priest saw Balda coming, he jumped up and hid behind his wife, shaking with fear and rage. Balda pulled him out, and handed him the ransom money in its heavy sack. Then, he demanded his reward.

At the first rap on the head, the priest flew up to the ceiling.

With the second rap, he was struck dumb.

And at the third, he lost his wits entirely.

And Balda said, reproachfully: 'It isn't wise to try to take a man's labour for nothing!'

1830

THE TALE OF
A FISHERMAN AND
A GOLDEN FISH

An old man lived with his wife in a ramshackle mud hut by the shores of a blue sea. They had lived there for thirty-three years. The old man was a fisherman, and used to cast his net for fish all day, while his wife spun her yarn. One day he cast out his net, but it came back full of nothing but slime. He threw the net out again – and it came back full of seaweed. A third time he threw out the net – and the net came back with a single fish in it: no ordinary fish, but a golden fish. The fish spoke to him in a human voice, pleading for its life: 'Throw me back into the sea, old man, and I will pay you a handsome price for my life – whatever you wish for I will grant.' The old man was amazed and frightened; for thirty-three years he had been a fisherman, and never had he heard a fish that could speak. He freed the golden fish, and said to him gently: 'Go peacefully, fish of gold! There is no need to pay me a ransom for your life. Go back to the blue sea, and splash in your freedom to your heart's content.'

The old man returned to his wife and told her about this extraordinary thing: 'I caught a fish today; not an ordinary one, but a golden fish. It spoke to me in our language, begging to return to the sea alive, and offering a rich price – to grant anything I wanted. I didn't dare ask it for a ransom, so I just let it go back into the sea.' The old woman began to scold her husband: 'You old fool, you great simpleton . . . you couldn't even take a reward from a fish? At least you might have asked for a new wash-trough, since ours is split right through.'

So the fisherman went back to the beach, and he saw that the water was slightly ruffled. He began to call the golden fish, and it came swimming up to him and asked: 'What is it that you need, old man?' With a low bow, the old man replied: 'Forgive me, good fish. My wife is scolding me, she won't leave me in peace: she needs a new wash-trough, since ours is completely split.' And the fish answered: 'Go home, and don't worry. The new wash-trough will be yours.' The old man went back to his wife, and already she had a new trough. But she began to scold him more than ever: 'What a simpleton you are! What a fool, to ask for just a wash-trough . . . what's a trough worth? Go back to the fish again; bow down to him, and ask him for a cottage for us.'

The fisherman went back again to the sea. (The water was becoming dim and troubled.) He called the golden fish, who swam up to him and asked: 'What do you need now, old man?' The old man bowed and replied: 'Forgive me, good fish – my wife is scolding me worse than before, and gives me no peace . . . the old shrew wants a cottage to live in.' The golden fish answered: 'Don't be troubled. The cottage will be yours.' So he went back to his old hut, but it was no longer there: before him stood a cottage with a white-washed brick chimney, and gates made of oak planks. The old woman was sitting by the window. As soon as she saw her husband she began to swear at him: 'What a fool you are! You idiot, you asked for nothing more than a cottage! Go back again, and bow low to the fish – I don't want to be a simple peasant any longer, I want to be a gentlewoman.'

The old man went back to the blue sea (which had lost its calm). He began to call the golden fish. The fish swam up to him and asked: 'What do you need now, old man?' With a bow the old man answered: 'Be patient, good fish. My old wife swore at me more than ever, and gives me no peace, old man though I am.

Now she says she will no longer be a peasant, but wants to be a gentlewoman.' The golden fish answered: 'Go home in peace, and don't worry.' The old man returned again to his wife, and saw in front of him – a tall stone mansion. In the porch stood his wife, dressed in an expensive padded jacket with sable collar, a brocade head-dress on her head, her neck laden with pearls, gold rings on her hands, and on her feet red satin slippers. Servants cowered before her; she was beating them, and pulling their hair. The old man spoke to his wife: 'Gentle lady, I think your wishes must be satisfied now.' The old woman only screeched at him, and sent him away to work in the stables.

So a week passed, and then another. The old woman behaved more and more ruthlessly, and again she sent the old man to the golden fish. 'Go to him again, and bow low. Tell him that I don't want to be just a gentlewoman now – I want to be a queen.' The old man was frightened, and implored her to be reasonable: 'What's wrong with you, old lady? Have you gone crazy? You don't even know how to talk or behave properly – you'll be the laughing stock of the whole kingdom.' The old woman was enraged. She slapped the old man on the face, and shouted: 'How dare you argue with me, old fool . . . with me a gentlewoman. Go back to the sea, I tell you – and if you won't go I will have you dragged there by force.'

The poor old man went back again to the sea-shore. The blue sea had turned completely black. He began to call the golden fish. The fish swam up to him, and asked: 'What do you need now, old man?' 'Forgive me, good fish,' the old man replied. 'My wife is being very difficult. She's already dissatisfied with being a gentle-woman, and she wants to be a mighty queen.' The golden fish

'Forgive me good fish. My wife is scolding me, she won't leave me in peace'

answered, again: 'Go back in peace, and do not worry. Very well! The old woman shall be a queen.'

The old man returned to his wife. Now, before him, stood a royal palace. Inside he saw his wife, sitting at a banquet table like a queen. She was eating honey-cakes, with nobles and gentlemen paying court to her, pouring her rare foreign wines. Fierce guards stood around the hall, with hatchets raised high on their shoulders. When the old man saw her, he was filled with terror. He bowed at his wife's feet, and said imploringly: 'Mighty queen: now, surely, all your wishes are fulfilled.' His wife didn't even look at him; with just a glance she ordered him to be taken away. The gentlemen and nobles rushed at him, and bundled and jostled the old man outside. The guards ran to the doorways, and only just avoided hacking him with their great axes. Outside, the people jeered at him: 'It serves you right, you old dunce! Here's a lesson to you in future, just to keep in your own place.'

So a week, and then another, passed. The old woman became still more demanding; she sent her courtiers out to find her husband, and they searched for him and brought him to her. 'Go back again, and bow low to the fish,' the old woman said to him. 'I no longer wish to be a queen – I will be the empress of the seas, and live in the deep ocean, so that the golden fish will be mine, to serve me and obey my commands.'

The old man did not dare to contradict her, and risk her fury. He went off to the blue sea, and saw a dark tempest over the water, and saw how the angry waves swelled and crashed. He began to call the golden fish, who swam up to him and asked: 'What do you need now, old man?' 'Forgive me, good fish!' answered the old man. 'What am I to do with this woman? She doesn't want to be a queen any longer, but demands to be the empress of the seas, and live in the deep ocean, and have you to serve her and do her bidding.'

The fish said nothing. With a flick of its golden tail, it disappeared into the deep sea.

For a long time the old man waited by the water for an answer, but none came. Slowly he returned to the old woman. The old mud hut stood as it had done, and in the doorway sat his wife. At her feet lay the broken wash-trough.

1833

The old mud hut stood as it had done, and in the doorway sat his wife. At her feet lay the broken wash-trough